Operation Discovery

Who, What, When, Where, & More In New Home Sales

Operation Discovery

Who, What, When, Where, & More In New Home Sales

Steve Hoffacker

CAPS, MCSP, MIRM

Operation Discovery

Who, What, When, Where & More In New Home Sales

Cover photo by Steve Hoffacker.

ALL RIGHTS RESERVED.

© 2010 by Hoffacker Associates LLC
West Palm Beach, Florida, USA

ISBN: 978-0-9843524-2-5

———

Each new home customer has different needs, interests, requirements, budgets, expectations, and motivations that may not be immediately obvious or apparent when you first meet them. Therefore, you must ask each customer a series of questions, in a professional and conversational way, to learn how to help them — and ultimately build and make a sale.

———

Other New Home Sales Books By Steve Hoffacker

To find additional books on new home sales written by Steve Hoffacker, visit http://stevehoffacker.com/new homesalesbooks.html.

Titles are available in print (softbound) and as Kindle eBooks, and they include:

"Making The Grade: *The A-B-C's Of Rating New Home Customers*"

"Selling With Builders: *How Realtors® Can Profit From Selling Builders' New Homes*"

"Using Your Network: *Making New Home Sales With People You Already Know*"

"Making New Friends: *Connecting With Strangers To Make More New Home Sales*"

"Universal Design For Builders: *Building & Selling Accessible, Safe & Comfortable New Homes*"

"Creating A Great First Impression: *Being An Effective New Home Sales Center Receptionist*"

"Fueling Your New Home Sales Business: *Making Strategic Contacts For More Sales & Referrals*"

Table Of Contents

Preface

I appreciate that you bought this book and that you are interested in being an even better new home salesperson than you are right now.

Each customer who visits your model home or new home sales center or contacts you for information is different.

People have various needs, interests, requirements, budgets, preferences, lifestyles, timetables, and abilities to act — and it's up to you to figure out what these are.

No one will walk into your office wearing a sign or handing you a card with their profile on it.

You will need to conduct a skillful interview with your customers to learn what their needs are and how you can help them.

Of course, some people will have a more immediate need than others to select their new home.

Some will be ready to make a decision on their new home during their initial visit, but most people will take at least a couple of visits before they feel comfortable in making a decision to acquire a new home.

Some will need help sorting through all the various opportunities available to them and determining which builder they want to work with for their new home.

Some may visit you several times and never make a decision — others are just "looking for decorating ideas."

Others will have a very hard time imagining themselves living in one of your new homes because of their needs, requirements, or expectations.

So how do you figure out what people are looking for in a new home and which ones are serious about getting a new home?

Start by asking appropriate questions in a conversational way and eliciting opinions, likes, dislikes, needs, requirements, preferences, and impressions.

Then you can begin to act on what people have told you and help them achieve their dreams.

"Discovery" — the process of asking a variety of questions to determine someone's needs and ability to act — is much like a reporter composing a story.

You need to ask a series of questions during your face-to-face presentation with someone to learn the "who," "what," "when," "where," "why," "how," and "which" of what they are seeking as they shop for a new home.

You also can use yes/no questions ("Do you like this homesite?" or "Is this what you had in mind?") — but often these questions don't give you enough information to work with.

To be in the best position to help your customers, you need to get them involved in expressing their opinions and sharing their attitudes with you by asking them questions than go beyond just a short answer.

When customers come to you, they have various needs, requirements, and capacities to make a decision — it's up to you to find out what those are.

By asking questions skillfully, you can determine how to help people find what they are seeking — and make more sales in the process.

Asking your customers questions about their needs is completely different than just offering a few trite pleasantries, such as "Hi, can I help you?" or "Would you like to see the model?"

You are dealing with one of the most important decisions in the lives of your customers, and you need to be ready to accept this responsibility.

You must skillfully guide them through the many issues and considerations that will affect and impact their decision.

This is where knowing how to ask the appropriate questions — and how to ask them in a variety of ways — will make you an effective communicator and an outstanding new home salesperson.

There are many ways of asking the same type of question — or for obtaining similar information — and we'll take a look at some of those in this book.

Operation Discovery

Who, What, When, Where, & More In New Home Sales

———

1

———

Who?

———

A Straightfoward Beginning

You are in the people business, so when someone enters your sales center, emails you, or calls for information, the first thing that matters — before you learn anything else — is who the person is that has contacted you.

You want their name.

Then you can begin learning other details.

The "who" question is different than all of the other questions that you'll ask your customers.

It has nothing to do with their opinions, preferences, wants, needs, expectations, or anything else of a qualitative nature.

This type of question calls for a factual response and will yield a specific name or a relationship — or both.

Getting Their Name

The best way to obtain the name or names of your customers is to offer yours first as you are greeting them and shaking hands with them (or as you are introducing yourself — if it's on the phone or by email).

Many times your customers will reflexively provide their names in response to your introduction. If they don't, it's simple enough to ask for their names at that point.

For instance, when you're shaking hands with your new customers — and they don't offer their names in response to you providing yours — simply hold onto their hand for a moment longer and ask *"And you are?"* or *"And your name is?"*

Then listen carefully for what they say and repeat it aloud.

Writing It Down

Write down everyone's first and last name on your information card — with the correct spelling and pronunciation. If they use a nickname, note it as well.

Even if you use a computer to store your customer records, make a note of the names and other important information on paper first and then transfer them to your database later.

Make sure to obtain the names of everyone present in the customer unit (regardless of age or relationship) so that you can include them — directly and specifically by name — in your presentation and your Follow-Through® contact.

Learning The Correct Spelling

How will you know if you have the correct spelling of their names? Don't guess. Don't write down what you think they are saying. You need to ask.

Often names sound alike but are spelled quite differently.

Take a name that sounds to you like *"Meyer."* It can also be *"Myer,"* or *"Meijer,"* or *"Maier,"* or *"Mayer,"* or *"Majer,"* or *"Myers,"* or *"Meyers,"* or *"Moyers,"* or *"Mires,"* or *"Miers,"* or *"Meijers."*

Even a common sounding surname such as *"Johnson"* could also be spelled *"Johnston"* or *"Johnstone"* or *"Jonson"* or *"Jonsen"* — and there are even more variations with first names, depending on nationality, gender, personal preference, and other factors.

Many first names can be used by either men or women. Sometimes they're spelled differently (such as *"Tony,"* or *"Toni,"* or *"Terry,"* or *"Teri"*), and many times they aren't.

Don't rely on what you *think* you hear. Ask.

When someone tells me their name is *"Johnson,"* I ask them *"Is that with or without the 't'?"* or I ask *"Is that J-o-h-n-s-o-n?"*

How's That Pronounced?

How will you know if you are pronouncing their last names correctly? Or their first names? Or the name of someone who is part of the decision but absent on the initial meeting?

Whether it's the first name or last — or both — you don't want to risk irritating or alienating your customers, or starting off your presentation poorly, by messing up how you say their names.

Begin by repeating each name after you hear it and then immediately write them down, spelled correctly — first and last names.

Your customers either will acknowledge that you have said their names properly or they will politely correct you. They will help you because they want to hear their names said correctly.

After you are sure that you are hearing their names correctly, make notes on your information card as to how to say them properly, and then say their names aloud again (using your notes as a key) — just to make sure that you have it right.

The Household Size

After you complete the introductions and learn the name or names of your customers — and write them down and know that you are pronouncing each name correctly — move on to determining the household size.

This is more important than just how many people will be living in the home or how many people are standing in front of you.

It helps you learn how many people may need to be involved in the decision as well as who the specific individuals are — even if they aren't all present.

This is *key* to making a sale.

You must know who you are working with and how each person in a particular customer unit factors into the decision-making process in order for you to be effective and successful.

Regardless of how many people are standing in front of you at the time, you ultimately need to determine exactly who your total customer unit is and how many people are involved in the decision.

The customer unit may be more than just the people who are going to be living in the new home you are discussing with them.

The Total Customer Unit

The total customer unit is the person, couple, family, or group — collectively — that you initially talk to about your homes that eventually makes the purchasing decision or influences it.

It can be a single person all the way to an extended family. It's up to you to determine how large the customer unit is, how it's constituted, and who everyone is that's a member of it.

For instance, the customer might be alone and be an unmarried single person, a person without their spouse or partner, or a single parent without children present — regardless of how many people are part of the decision.

It could be a male-female couple — either a married or unmarried couple with no children, none to occupy their new home on a regular basis, or with children not present with them at the initial meeting.

It could be a traditional husband-wife family with young children, school-age children, teenagers, or a mixture of ages present with them — or additional children of various ages at home.

You might be working with another type of couple, such as two unmarried but related individuals (mother or father and an adult child, sisters, brothers, or cousins, for example) or two unrelated friends — regardless of apparent age differences or whether children are involved or not.

Then, there are the aunts, uncles, parents, grandparents, adult children and siblings, best friends, financial planners, attorneys, and others who may advise or impact the decision.

The Fair Housing Act

Ultimately, you need to know who you're working with and how they might be related to each other — if at all.

You can introduce yourself to your customers and learn their names, but you can't assume anything about their relationships or family status — regardless of how it might appear to you.

You definitely can't come right out and ask either.

You need to have them volunteer this information for you, and then you can talk about it with them.

The Fair Housing Act doesn't permit questions about relationships, marital status, or family size.

You can't ask anything that will appear to be discriminatory or suggest that anyone is or will be treated any differently than another.

While this is not your intention, it's still off limits.

You just want to get a better idea of who you are working with, but it could be construed that you will show homes to people or discuss your opportunities with them based on the way that they answer your questions.

That's why such questions are not allowed.

When There's Only One Person

Let's take a fairly common case that may be easy to misjudge.

When someone comes into your model home or sales center alone, do you have a tendency to assume that they have a spouse or partner they will need to consult, or do you assume that they are unmarried?

An unaccompanied person entering in your sales center doesn't mean that they are single — and it doesn't mean that they aren't. That's the point.

You can't tell about someone's marital status just by looking (whether they are wearing rings or not), and you can't come right out and ask them if they are married — or say anything about a spouse or partner.

Nevertheless, you need to learn if there are other decision-makers or influencers involved.

Are Others Involved?

In the case of an unaccompanied person, you need to determine for yourself if anyone else needs to be included or involved in looking at the property, or if they will be assisting your unaccompanied customer in their decision — but you can't ask if they are married or if they have children.

You can ask if anyone else might be a party to the decision or if they'll need to consult with someone else, but you can't establish or ask for the nature of that relationship until it is mentioned.

When they volunteer information about relationships or family members, you then can talk about it and discuss how other people that they mention might be involved in the buying decision.

Just remember that you can't be the one to ask for this information or to introduce it into the conversation.

You can just determine if they are making the decision by themselves or if others will be involved.

Are They Looking For Themselves?

Begin by asking a person that is unaccompanied if they are looking for a home for themselves. This question doesn't imply anything.

Regardless of how they answer your question, you then want to learn if other people might be involved in the decision — or if they plan to consult with others or return with them before making a purchasing decision.

Examples of such questions that you can ask include *"Are you looking for something for yourself?"* or *"Will this home be just for you?"* or *"Are you the one looking for (interested in) a new home?"*

You can also ask *"Will there be someone else (Is anyone else) helping you make a decision (on your new home)?"* or *"Is there anyone else involved in helping you make a decision on your new home?"*

This does not suggest that someone else will need to be involved or that you assume them to be married or to have a family — or that you are inferring that they are incapable of making a decision on their own. It is simply a confirmation question.

If they say that they are single, fine. However, you still need to know about other people who may be involved in the decision.

This could be children (either children at home or adult children), a fiancé/fiancée, parents, siblings, a friend, other relatives, a financial advisor, or an attorney — even if none of those people actually will be occupying the residence with your customer.

On the other hand, if they say that they are looking for a new home along with their spouse, friend, family, or children as well, then you may ask for the names of those other individuals and a little bit about their needs and interests. Be sure to write down the information on your card — along with the correct spelling.

When Two People Are Together

When two men, two women, or a man and a woman enter your model center *together*, they might appear to have some type of relationship — but you cannot assume anything.

Relationships aren't always as they seem.

You need to clarify who you are working with and identify the decision-makers to proceed with your presentation effectively.

They might be related in some way, and they might not.

One of them might just be "tagging along" with the other — while that person is house-hunting.

Just as you would with a person who is alone, you need to ask a clarifying question when two people are present together, such as, *"Are you looking for something for the two of you?"* or *"Will this home be for just the two of you?"*

Again, there's the question about outside help: *"Will there be anyone else helping you make a decision?"* or *"Is there anyone else who will be (involved in) helping you make a decision on your new home?"*

As I said before, this doesn't assume or imply that they will need help or that they are incapable of making a decision without the input and participation of others. It's simply for clarification and confirmation.

Family Size Can't Be Assumed

Even if two people appear to be husband and wife or introduce themselves to you in that way, you can't make any assumptions about family size or anyone else who might be participating in the decision.

Regardless of their age, they might be relying on the opinions, advice, or contributions of children, parents, friends, relatives, or other advisors.

If two men (or two women) come into your model center together, one of them might be looking for a new home with their friend (who is just there to accompany the other one), or they could be looking for a home to occupy together — whether they are related or not.

Each could be looking separately for a new home — to occupy alone or with others — and just decided to visit your model center together.

If they happen to be related in some way, such as brothers, sisters, cousins, parent and adult child, grandparent and grandchild, nephew and uncle, niece and aunt, brothers-in-law, or sisters-in-law, they still might not intend to occupy the new home together.

Nothing Can Be Assumed

The point is you just don't know how — or if — people are related to each other, how they will occupy a new home, how many people will be living in the new home, or who might be making or influencing the decision.

You can't assume anything. Always keep this in mind.

You must ask questions.

You need to learn who is interested in the new home, who is making the decision, who might be an influencing or consulting party to the decision, and who will be occupying the new home.

You must find out who in your customer unit is making or influencing the purchasing decision so that you can focus on making your presentation to include the appropriate person or individuals.

This is true whether any or all of these other influential people are present at your initial meeting. In fact, you might not ever meet or speak with them.

The "Influencers"

The "influencers" definitely have to be taken into consideration to build a sale. They are the silent, sometimes missing, part of the total customer unit — people that you may never meet or see.

They won't be occupying the new home, but they definitely can impact the decision.

You always need to learn who the people are that you are working with directly, but it's essential that you also determine who else will be involved in the decision.

Knowing who these "influencers" are and how they factor into the decision might even be more important than knowing about the people in the customer unit.

There might be no one else involved in the decision other than people you meet.

However, if there are others, you need to include them in your presentation or ask about them in your Follow-Through® contact — even if you never meet or speak with these other people.

Remember that the age, apparent relationships, and the number of people present in your sales center are no indicators of how non-present influencers may be impacting or directing the decision.

Learning About The "Influencers"

Make it part of your early discovery questions to ask people about who will be assisting them in making the decision on their new home.

Ask questions like *"As you are looking for your new home, are there any other people you will want (need) to consult before making a decision?"* or *"Is there anyone else you will want to show (bring back to see) what you've selected (picked out) or consult with before you can decide (make a decision) (say 'yes') on your new home?"*

If there is no one else involved in the decision-making process, concentrate on working with the person or people in front of you.

Just be aware that they might try to use this later on in your presentation to forestall making a decision — saying that they need to check with someone else.

Identifying The "Influencers"

If your customers tell you that there is someone else (or even more than one other person) that will be assisting them with the decision — or people that they would like to consult before making a decision — learn specifically who these other people are (by name) and how they are related to your customers.

Determine generally where they live and why they are being consulted.

Try to learn specifically what it is that the influencers will be adding to the discussion.

Find out why their advice is being relied upon, the nature of their concern, and if they have any special background that makes their advice valuable.

Then focus on addressing these issues in your presentation and post-visit Follow-Through® contact.

Be sure to note who these influencers are.

Write their names on your information card, spell their names correctly, and add any pronunciation keys that you might need.

Show the names of any and all influencers on your card in parentheses — "(*names of missing people*)" — to indicate that there are such people that are going to be part of the overall decision.

Even if the person is not immediately identified by name but just by relationship — or even if that person is in a different part of the country or not even familiar with your location, note that person anyway the best way that you can ("*co-worker*," or "*friends from the office*," or "*cousin in Chicago*," or "*uncle in Philadelphia*").

The Broker As "Influencer"

Beyond family, friends, co-workers, and other advisors, there might be a broker or agent involved with your customers — particularly if it's a relocation to your area.

You need to know who this person is as well, plus any relationship that there might be — and be prepared to include them in the presentation.

If there is a long-standing relationship between your customers and the agent, they may be relying on their help for counsel. Learn about that, too.

The broker may not accompany their customers each time, but that doesn't mean their influence is missing.

If your customers tell you that there is no agent or anyone one else involved in helping them reach a decision, confirm it and proceed with your presentation.

Don't be overly concerned that your customers will try to mention someone else later on to delay their decision.

Selling To The Absent Influencers

If your customers mention other people who will be influencing their decision, be sure to include these other people in your presentation, using their names or relationships as you refer to them.

Make certain to specifically seek the approval of those influencers or decision-makers who are not present.

Ask your customers how well they think that their absent influencers might like something that you are showing them — or whether they would approve of it.

For instance, you might ask *"Is this the kind of home you think your cousin Bill would approve of (like, want) for you?"* or *"Is this the kind of home you think your sister Eileen has in mind for you?"* or *"What do you think your parents would say about this home for you?"*

If your customers are concerned about being able to accommodate their parents when they decide to visit, ask them *"How (How well) do you think your parents (in-laws, mother, mother-in-law) would like visiting you (staying with you, living here with you) in this home?"*

Other question possibilities are *"What do you think your wife/husband* (not present) *would say about this kitchen?"* or *"How do you think you and your wife/husband would use this family room (basement, deck, porch, bonus room, patio)?"* or *"How do you think Jimmy/Suzie* (not present) *would like this bedroom?"*

Or you could ask *"What type (style, size) of home do your parents think you should acquire?"* or *"Do you think that this is the type of home that your parents would like (approve of) for you to have?"* or *"Have you*

*discussed any of the other homes you've looked at with
your parents?"* or *"What have your parents had to say so
far about your search for a new home?"*

Avoiding Surprises With Influencers

Imagine working with someone for several minutes and
thinking that you are getting close to reaching an
agreement on a floor plan for them to own when they
mention that they need to discuss the whole issue of
getting a new home with someone else.

They act as if they're in control of the buying process as
they reflect on the floor plan you're showing them, but
they wait until well along in the presentation — maybe
even the very end — to mention the other person.

Until that moment, you didn't realize this unknown
person was a factor in the buying process, and your
customer is unwilling to proceed without the advice and
counsel of this other person.

Wouldn't it have been nice to know about this other
person at the beginning of your on-site presentation and
that they would factor into the decision?

This way, you could have tailored your presentation
toward appealing to those people that might participate
in or comment on the decision — and not have assumed
that you were talking with a decision-maker.

Sometimes people will tell you that there is no one else involved in the decision and then later say that they need to check with someone or talk to them as a way of buffering or diffusing your pursuit of the sale.

However, if you ask about other people early in your presentation, customers often will reveal the names or relationships of other people that will be part of the decision — particularly if they think that this will take the pressure off them so they can just look at the model.

Assuming There Is A Spouse

When salespeople are working with someone who is alone, I often see them make a serious blunder.

They mistakenly assume (without confirming how the decision will be made) that the customer is married and that they will need to check with their spouse before making a decision.

Clueless salespeople keep talking to the unaccompanied person about returning with their spouse — when often there isn't one because the customer is unmarried.

This means that the person who is present will be making the decision for himself or herself.

The person present is likely quite offended and turned off by the references and suggestions that they are not capable of a decision on their own, that they must be married, or that they need the help of a spouse to make a decision.

This means that making a sale in such cases is probably not very likely.

Never assume anything about someone's family size or their ability to make a decision without the influence of others.

You must get clarification. Misreading the situation could easily cost you a sale.

Assuming There Must Be A Family

At the other end of the spectrum, a man and woman may arrive together and have children with them — particularly younger children.

It may appear to be a family, but you cannot immediately assume that it is.

It likely is and very well could be a family situation, but it might be something else entirely.

Again, you need to clarify who you are working with.

Typically, it would be a husband and wife with their own children, but it could other situations as well.

It could be an unmarried couple with their own children. Then again, the children could belong to either the man or the woman, or some to each of them.

It also could be a husband and wife or unmarried couple with some of their own children and some of their children's friends or cousins.

The children could be other relatives of the adults, such as nieces, nephews, or grandchildren. This could be true even if the adults you are working with have other children who are not present with them.

When There Are Children Present

The presence of children often implies or suggests a family relationship, so when customers arrive in your sales center with children, you want to sort things out quickly so you'll be able to conduct an effective presentation.

A great way to begin learning who everyone is (including their names) — and possibly how they are related to each other — is to ask for introductions.

Ask the kids directly who they are by name (but not whose they are), or ask the adults to introduce you to all of the children present.

Don't ask about relationships — wait for it to be offered.

Usually the adults will indicate how the children are related to them and to each other — and mention any non-related children who might be present and how they happen to be there.

After learning this, you can ask about other people who might be members of the family but aren't present.

Parents love to talk about their children and generally will give you the information you need about ages and relationships when presented the opportunity.

When you learn who the children are, be sure to add their names to your information card — as well as noting the names of any who are not present.

Be aware that children present or at home may not have the same last name as their parents or guardians.

Identifying The Key Decision-Maker

Whether there are absent influencers or not, you also need to know who in your customer unit is the most influential or prominent decision-maker.

You must receive the approval from this person in order to actually make the sale.

Usually there is one person in a family who is the chief decision-maker or primary influencer — even if he or she isn't as vocal or doesn't participate in the conversation as much as some of the others.

In fact, he or she might not even be present on the initial visit to your model center.

Nevertheless, this is the person who ultimately will make the purchasing decision.

You can't directly ask this question, but as you are conducting your discovery and learning about your customers, you need to determine who the person is in the customer unit that you need to secure the "yes" from to signify an ownership decision.

This is the person you need to appeal to and make sure that they are comfortable with what you are offering — even if they are not present at the initial meeting.

You must secure the support, approval, and agreement of the primary decision-maker in order to make a sale.

Obtaining Referrals

Knowing who your customers are, including anyone else that might factor into their decision process, is the first part of building the sale.

We've talked about the importance of including brokers and absent influencers in your presentation — and the value of focusing on gaining the approval of the chief decision-maker.

Now, there is another big "who" of your discovery process that you'll want to learn.

You'll want to determine who else your customers know that *might* be interested in hearing about what you offer — as well as those they feel *definitely* would be interested in living in one of your new homes.

These questions can generate referrals as well as help the people you are working with to focus on the positive aspects of what you are offering — as they think of friends, relatives, co-workers, or neighbors that might like to know about your homes.

Even when people have decided that their needs cannot be met by what you are offering — or you determine that they are not in a position to make a decision in the near future — they still may know people that should hear about your opportunity. So ask.

Referrals are a big part of producing additional customers and capitalizing on your company's traffic generation and advertising investment.

It is something you can do to supplement your own lead generation program, and it costs absolutely nothing for you to ask for a referral.

Your customers are going to know people that you don't.

If you don't learn about other people through your customers, you won't have the opportunity to find out who they are and connect with them about your homes.

Using Testimonials From Friends

Another type of referral and a great "who" question that you can ask people during your discovery process is who they might know that already has looked at and considered your new homes.

Then determine what type of relationship exists between these people and your customers.

For instance, are they close friends, relatives, casual acquaintances, business associates, co-workers, friends-of-friends, or neighbors?

This is relying on a *reverse* type of referral where their friends may have prompted or influenced their current visit with you.

This can lead to a discussion of what their friends, relatives, or acquaintances have experienced and what they have told them about those experiences.

Sometimes people visiting you will have some familiarity with your company or what you build because they might have accompanied their friends or relatives when they were looking for a new home.

While not related to speaking to anyone about your homes, people can gain some familiarity in what you're offering from looking at your website before their visit.

Tapping Into Current Owners

A similar "who" question for your customers is who they know that currently lives in one of your homes or who is in the process of having one of your new homes built.

Of course, you'll want to know what these people have discussed with your customers — or told them about the homes you build and your quality and workmanship.

You'll also want to know the nature of the relationship that exists and how this might have prompted their visit.

Asking About Work Force

Another "who" question that might come up in conversation is who they know that might work for your company or one of your subs or suppliers.

Then you can find out what those people might have shared with them about their experiences in working for your company, the quality of the homes that you build, or how they think you compare to the competition.

You can draw out the conversation by asking specifically what those people do who work for your suppliers or trades, how long they have been doing it, and how they feel about their contributions to your homes.

Discussing Your Competition

Still another important "who" question involves your competition and the marketplace.

Get in the practice of asking your customers who else they have looked at (other builders) — and why.

Learn how what they've seen compares to what they are experiencing with you and also how it has met or failed to address their needs.

Determine what you might be able to do to compete more favorably with the competition.

Finding out about your competition and your marketplace is one of the ways to achieve a return on your traffic generation and advertising investment — even when no sale ever results.

Make it a practice to ask everyone that visits your sales center questions about what they have experienced in the marketplace. Learn how they feel it compares or contrasts to what you offer and what they are looking for in a new home.

Don't forget to ask your customers who else they are still planning on looking at or considering. Then you can explore why.

More Than Just Introductions

In short, there are plenty of "who" questions that you should know the answers to as you begin your presentation.

These will help you get to know the wants and needs of your customers.

Again, not everything you ask needs to include the word "who" in the question — but your customers need to supply that type of information in the response.

Asking "who" questions is much more than just learning the names of people who are standing in front of you.

As we have discussed, learning who people are and how to pronounce their names correctly is very important, but it's only the first step.

The same holds true for people that you are "meeting" by telephone and email.

You start by learning the names of anyone who walks into your sales center or model home — or those who telephone you or contact you by email.

Then you move on to the many other important "who" issues and questions that you will use to build relationships and ultimately make sales.

Remember Those Influencers

Don't forget the importance of the non-present influencers. Learn who they are so that you can include them by direct reference in your presentation and explore their opinions and comments.

Be mindful of the tremendous impact that friends, relatives, advisors, real estate sales professionals, associates, influencers, and others can have on the eventual decision, and work to understand how to win their approval.

Remember that the most important influencer of all in making the decision is going to be the major decision-maker in the customer unit.

You must identify this person and specifically sell to him or her.

2

What?

Expressing Opinion Or Fact

Asking or using a "what" question seems so basic — and
it is.

That's because it can express either an opinion or a fact
— as in *"What do you think?"* (opinion) or *"What is the
answer?"* (fact).

As you meet your customers for the first time — in
person, over the telephone, or online — and you begin to
learn a little about them, of course you'll want to know
who you are talking to.

As we discussed in the last chapter, getting their names
and learning more about who they are is quite
important.

Along with that, you'll need to know what they want,
and what it will take to sell them a new home.

What Are They Looking For?

There are many ways to ask people what they're looking for in a new home, floor plan, or layout.

To get the "what" process started, you might begin by asking a general introductory question, such as *"What are you looking for (in a new home)?"* or *"What type of home are you looking for?"* or *"What are you looking for today?"* or *"What did (do) you have in mind for your new home?"*

You can use a statement, such as *"Tell me about what you're looking for (in a new home opportunity, layout, floor plan),"* or *"Tell me about your needs,"* or *"Describe what you have in mind for your new home,"* or *"Tell me (Describe) what you're thinking about in terms of (for) your new home."*

"Breaking The Ice"

This first "what" question is a very simple introductory one. It's asked as much to break-the-ice (like a *"how are you?"* question does) as it is to get a definitive answer from your customers.

While you'd like to learn the specific type of home they want, or at least get a general idea of the size, layout, price, or design, you may only get a non-focused response when you ask this question.

Some people have a more definite idea of what they want in a new home than others. Some only know what they don't want.

They may say something like *"We're not really sure,"* or *"We don't know, we just started looking,"* or *"It's kind of early in the process so we don't really know yet,"* or *"We really don't know what's available."*

They could say *"We'll know it when we see it,"* or *"It's kind of hard to describe,"* or *"It all depends on what we see (find),"* or *"We're not really looking, but if we happen to see something we like ...."*

They may just say that they just are looking for something comfortable, affordable, or appealing that will meet their needs — without elaborating.

An Issue Of Communication

Asking people *"What are you looking for in a new home?"* may seem like a question that can be answered relatively easily.

It seems like a factual response could be given, but we know that some people have trouble visualizing or verbalizing what they want.

Such a question, while simple to ask, can have many interpretations and responses from your customers.

It isn't so much what you think you are asking in this early discovery question.

What matters is what your customers *think* you are asking or think that you want to know about their new home search.

It may seem like a straightforward question that just asks people to explain what they are looking for in a new home.

Nevertheless, you may need to ask several additional questions before you get enough information to have more than just a generalized idea of what they want.

Be patient and help them to verbalize what they have in mind — even if they initially think that they can't express it.

Needing To Ask More Questions

Instead of a general *"what are you looking for?"* question, you may need to ask a more direct question.

For instance, *"What are you looking for in a floor plan (new home)?"* or *"What specifically are you looking for in a new home layout?"* or *"What type of new home are you looking for?"* or *"What does your new home need to have (in order) for it to meet your needs (requirements)?"*

Or you might ask *"What features are you looking for in a new home?"* or *"What features are important for you to have in a new home?"* or *"What type of floor plan do you have in mind?"* or *"What ideas do you have for a layout?"*

You could ask them to *"Describe what type of floor plan you're looking for (have in mind)."*

Other questions are *"Have you seen anything that is close to what you're looking for?"* or *"What have you seen anywhere that is close to what you're looking for?"* or *"What else have you been looking at in the area?"*

When People Aren't Expressive

Sometimes people just know that they would like to change from what they have now without knowing exactly where to begin.

However, some will intentionally be vague about what they want because they are more interested in looking at your model and getting a brochure than they are in actually talking with you.

Other times, they may have an idea of what they want — or maybe a better idea of what they *don't* want — but they just are having trouble putting it into words.

You may need to use their current home for reference.

Starting With Their Current Home

Here, skillful questioning is important as you ask about their current home and how they use it.

You don't want to put them on the defensive or give them the impression that you are ridiculing or minimizing their present home.

Don't ask them to defend why they chose that home. Just learn their likes and dislikes about it to give you some direction in helping them select a new home.

Start by determining what features they like or feel are the most important to them in their current home. Ask them *"What features in your current home are the most important to you?"*

Learn what features they use the most or find the most helpful or beneficial and which ones they'd like to have in a new home if they could — regardless of how feasible it might be or the actual price of doing it.

You also can ask them what rooms or areas of their present home are the most important to them (in terms of where they spend most of their waking time or where their family tends to gather) and what they definitely would like to have in a new home (based on what features they've already identified or decided as being necessary or important for them to have).

Re-Designing Their Current Home

Ask your customers *"If you could redesign your present home to make it more ideal for your current situation, what would you do (do differently)?"* or *"If you could change anything about your current home, what would you do?"*

You can ask *"What features are missing from your current home that you think would make your lives more comfortable or easier?"* or *"What features that you like in your current home do you want to take with you (include) in your new home?"*

The converse of this would be *"What features in your current home are not that important to you now?"* or *"What features in your current home would you just as soon not have in your new home?"*

Similarly, you can ask *"What aspects of your current home would you definitely want to have in a new home as well?"* or *"If you could start over by designing a new home for yourselves, what features would you include in it, and which rooms would you say are the most important to you?"*

Obviously, they *can* start over with a new home so this line of questioning can be very revealing in terms of what's important to them and what areas you need to focus on to make a sale.

This type of questioning really gets your customers involved in the discussion and is especially helpful when people seem to have difficulty in describing or verbalizing what they're looking for in a new home.

Picking The Homesite

There's also the homesite or the location issue. This is a big "what" question for you and your customers. There can't be a sale without a specific location.

When it comes time for your customers to look at and pick out a specific homesite or location for their new home, what do they have in mind as far as size, orientation, general setting, or specific physical features?

Again, you are seeking a factual response when you ask questions such as *"What type of homesite are you looking for?"* or *"What did you have in mind as far as a homesite?"* or *"What kinds of features are important for you to have in a homesite?"*

However, your customers may not have thought that much about the type of homesite they want, or they might not know what's available. Then again, they might have a very specific idea of what they want.

You may need to ask more than one question to identify the type of homesite to show them.

For instance, depending on the choices that you offer, you can ask if they want something relatively level, one that is wooded or has several trees, something that backs up to the preserve or open space, a waterfront location, something relatively private, something on a corner, a zero-premium site regardless of other attributes, or one that has some special interest such as its configuration or topography.

Choosing The Neighborhood

In asking what someone is looking for in a new home, you also want to know what type of neighborhood or community they are seeking.

Are they looking for active recreational activities such as golf, tennis, swimming, or fitness? Are they looking for a clubhouse, dining, and game rooms? For a gated community with a secure entrance?

Are they seeking more passive interests such as trails and sidewalks for walking, jogging, or skating?

How about activities for the children?

Are they looking for a 55+ adult community?

Other aspects of a community may be even more important than what it offers, such as its natural setting or its proximity to local services and facilities.

Many people are interested in commuting routes and how easy it is to get to and from their new home and work, school, and other regular activities.

Distance to the airport often is important.

Mixing Up The Questions

In asking discovery questions to learn about "what," you don't necessarily have to use the specific word "what" in the question.

The questions just need to be formed in such a way that they will yield these types of responses and tell you what people are seeking or requiring.

Sometimes the word "what" will appear in your questions, but the questions may not begin with that word or even include it in the phrasing — this way you'll provide some variety to your "what" questions.

For instance, you might ask *"Are you looking for ...?"* or *"How important is ...?"* or *"Is that what you are looking for?"* or *"Is that the kind of home you are looking for?"* or *"Is that what you are interested in?"*

All of these questions will give you a direct "what" response — or help you clarify what your customers are looking for or find important — as you continue to have a conversation with them.

You could also ask them to *"Describe what you are looking for,"* or *"Tell me what you have in mind."*

Confirming Product Type

If you offer a mixture of product types, you want to learn what type or style of home your customers are looking for.

Even if you are building just one product type, such as all single-family, townhomes, or high-rise condominium residences, you need to confirm that your customers are interested in what you offer so you don't spend time showing them something that they don't want.

Sometimes people will visit you without a clear idea of the type or style of home that you build — or the price range.

Before you get too far into describing your community or your homes — or assuming that people know what you offer — clarify that your customers are looking for what you are building.

You also can learn about what they're looking for by finding out what they've already been looking at in the marketplace.

For instance, *"What other communities have you seen (visited)?"* or *"What other builders have you visited?"*

Additional possibilities are *"What else have you looked at so far?"* or *"What other homes have you looked at?"* or *"What types of homes have you been looking at (considering)?"*

You also can ask *"Have you seen anything yet that is close to what you are looking for?"* or *"What have you seen so far that is close to what you are looking for?"*

Learning About Their Expectations

"What" questions are great for learning about the expectations of your customers so that you can adapt your presentation to address their needs — and determine what to highlight in your presentation.

Ask questions such as *"What made you decide to visit us today?"* or *"What would you like to accomplish today?"* or *"In our limited time together today, what would you like to accomplish (focus on) while you are here?"*

Other questions are *"How can I use your time the most effectively today?"* or *"What are you most interested in seeing or learning about today?"* or *"What is the most important thing for you to find out about today?"*

You don't want to verbalize such a question in front of your customers, but you need to ask yourself the same type of question: *what do you want to accomplish during your time with them?*

Getting Onto Their Short List

If it's the initial visit for your customers, at a minimum you need to present a strong case as to why your company should be a finalist as the builder they would select for their new home. This is the "what" that you need to accomplish.

Even if your customers won't admit it, they are taking stock of you, your company, and what you offer to determine if they want to do business with you.

They are interviewing you as much as you are interviewing them.

Thus, your primary objective during your initial presentation with someone is to convince them that you are worthy of their continued interest.

This is the all-important *"justification"* phase of your overall sales process, and this is what I term *"making it onto their short list."*

If this is a return visit, you are that much closer to making a sale and should determine exactly what remains to be accomplished before that can happen.

Most sales happen after the initial visit, so that won't be possible unless you make it onto their short list and then remain on it as they narrow their choices.

When The End Comes Too Soon

You certainly want to make it onto your customer's short list and provide justification as to how you and your company can meet their needs — and that you're worthy of remaining as a finalist in their search for a new home.

However, sometimes you may not get a complete opportunity to present your case.

Your customers might have a time constraint, or something could come up that brings a hasty and premature end to your presentation.

Thus, as you move along through your presentation, you need to constantly assess what you have accomplished with each customer to that point (during that particular presentation and historically — if this is not the initial conversation) and what needs to happen next.

This is especially important for those times when your presentation ends abruptly before you reach a normal stopping point or conclusion.

If your presentation is terminated early, you must determine what remains to be done, discussed, or shown — and then convey that to your customer.

Your presentation won't always "run its course" and reach a planned, natural conclusion.

Being Prepared For An Abrupt Ending

There will be times when you are interrupted, when an emergency occurs, or when your customer abruptly stops your presentation and tells you that they need to leave.

You must be prepared for this to happen and know what you want or need to do next with a particular customer when it happens. Then you must get quick agreement from your customer for it to occur.

Also, there are plenty of times when a customer will come in just to get a brochure or look at your models quickly — with essentially no presentation by you.

Other times, you may begin a presentation with someone only to discover that they need to leave for an appointment or that they need to pick up their kids from school, practice, or a lesson.

It could be something disruptive as well, such as when their kids become fussy or unruly or complain of not feeling well. It might even be you or your customer who may not be feeling well. It could be something like a power outage also.

Your customer might get a cell phone call that causes them to cut their visit short — or you could be the one called away to meet with another customer who has a more immediate need, or to attend to an emergency.

Knowing What You Want To Do Next

What do you do in these "hurry-up" cases, and what do you recommend to your customers in each instance as the next step of activity?

What do you still need to accomplish with each customer?

Even when your presentation ends normally — when you had covered all that you had planned to discuss or mentioned everything that was feasible for you to talk about for that visit — what remains to be done?

What do you want to do next?

What will it take for them to make a decision?

These are powerful "what" questions that you need to answer to be in control of your sales process.

You need to have ready answers for these questions, and you need to know how to make such a quick assessment for each customer.

Asking About Work Or School

Now, for some additional questions that you'll want to ask or explore with your customers. This will help you work with them more effectively.

Ask your customers about their occupations or professions with such questions as *"What do you do (for a living)?"* or *"What is your occupation (profession)?"* or *"Where do you work? What do you do there? How long have you been doing it?"*

You can continue with questions or observations like *"What aspects of your work do you really enjoy?"* or *"What do you like best about your job (position, profession)?"* or *"What's the most interesting thing about (satisfying part of, rewarding aspect of) your work?"* or *"That sounds very interesting."* or *"I'll bet that's interesting (fun, rewarding) work."*

If they are retired, ask what occupations or professions they had while they were working. You can also ask them what they enjoy doing now that they are retired. Do they do any type of volunteer work? What is their passion?

When children are present, you can ask them similar questions.

Depending on their ages, you can ask them *"What school do you go to (attend)?"* or *"What grade are you in (going into)?"* or *"What kinds of activities are you in at school?"* or *"Do you play sports?"* or *"What subjects do you enjoy?"* or *"What college are you planning on attending?"* or *"What do you plan on (are you) majoring in at college?"*

Establishing Common Ground

Questions about their employment or school activities let you learn a little more about your customers and help you connect with them.

They allow you to establish and explore some common ground with your customers — especially if you have a similar background, children of that age, a related work experience, a shared recreational interest, or know someone with a similar background, such as an immediate family member, neighbor, or close friend.

People like discussing personal experiences or talking about themselves, and if you can speak their language as it relates their profession or hobby, you will help them feel more at ease.

Many times, you just have to ask a good question and then just listen as they share a wealth of information about their experiences, likes, dislikes, needs, and requirements.

You also can relate to them that some of your homeowners are similarly employed (or used to be before they retired), or that they enjoy similar hobbies and activities.

This information also can help you form an economic snapshot of what they might be able to afford.

Learning About Special Conditions

There might be special issues in the lives of your customers that need to be resolved before a decision can occur.

These could be family (personal) or economic (financial) issues that mitigate the ability of your customers to focus on getting a new home and forestall any decision.

You should use "what" questions to learn about and explore them.

For instance, there may be important family considerations (such as long-term medical conditions, an unexpected death in the family, a recent cancer diagnosis, pending surgery, an injury, or an acute illness) that might affect someone's timing or ability to make a decision.

You might learn about these conditions or issues when you first meet someone, but most likely, you will learn about them during your continuing Follow-Through® contact with your customers.

Some May Be Economic Factors

There also could be economic challenges such as loss of a job, pending layoff, work stoppage, recent bankruptcy, repossessions, unforeseen major expenses (medical bills, auto repairs, or home maintenance and repairs), late payments, college tuitions or student loans, low credit scores, or high credit card debt.

Often other demands on the customer's finances — short or long-term — can impact, interrupt, derail, or deter their intended or anticipated home purchase.

Learn what these issues are and how they are impacting your customers and their new home search.

You need to be sensitive to these and do your best to help people see past them and look forward to actual home ownership with you.

It may take time to work through these issues, and you may or may not be able to help your customers resolve them and continue with their planned home purchase.

So in addition to learning what the issues are, you need to determine what it will take for your customers to resolve or work through these challenges — or what you can do to assist them in putting those issues behind them so that they can focus on owning their new home.

Asking Financial Questions

A huge "what" question — and one that is frequently overlooked or ignored — is the one about money and what people can afford to invest in a new home.

There is a tendency to think that this topic is "off-limits" and that only the lender can go here.

However, you need a general idea of what someone can afford and their general credit-worthiness as far as the likelihood of them getting a loan.

Begin with the investment amount, *"What are you thinking of investing in your new home?"* or *"Do you have an amount that you are trying to stay within as far as the total investment in your new home?"* or *"What had you thought about as far as your total investment in your new home?"*

"What have you budgeted for your new home?" or *"What's a comfortable amount for you to invest in your new home?"* can also be asked.

You can ask *"Have you met with (talked with, sat down with) a lender to discuss (determine, talk about, look into) how much home you can afford (qualify for, purchase)?"* or *"What amount have (had) you planned on spending on (investing in) your new home?"*

"Are you pre-qualified for a certain amount?"

Similarly, you can ask about the monthly investment with *"What are you thinking of as far as a monthly investment?"* or *"What do you have in mind for a monthly investment for your new home?"*

"Do you have an amount that you are trying to stay within as far as your total monthly investment?" or *"What kind of monthly figure did you have in mind for your new home?"*

Determine if that's just the principal and interest, the monthly escrow payment (including taxes and insurance), or the total monthly amount for everything — including association expenses.

To get started with the paperwork, ask *"What type of initial investment were you thinking of (planning on)?"* or *"What amount (How much) were you thinking of as far as an initial investment?"*

How Realistic Are They?

People may not know what they can afford, or they may be using a price point that is not realistic for what they say they want in a new home.

If they do state an amount that they are considering investing in a new home, learn how they determined that amount or how they arrived at that figure.

They may just be picking a number because it sounds nice compared to what they have now, they saw something in that price range that appealed to them, or a friend or relative bought something in this price range a few years ago when credit was easier to get.

Asking About Credit-Worthiness

Also, you want to know about their general credit history.

You don't need details, such as they missed a car payment because their daughter was in the hospital.

All you need to know is whether there are any late payments, short sales, foreclosures, repossessions, or other issues that might affect their credit score or ability to get financed easily.

Ask *"Is there anything that I (we) should know about that might affect your ability to get financing on your new home?"* or *"Is there anything in your credit report that we should be concerned about?"* or *"How would you describe your general credit rating (history)?"*

Most salespeople don't ask about credit history and then are surprised when someone can't qualify for a mortgage.

Isn't it better to learn sooner rather than later that there might be an issue getting your buyer financed?

Before sending someone to your lender, why not ask what the general state of their credit is and determine how likely it is that you can get them approved with your preferred lender?

Also, by knowing if there are any issues, you can select a lender who works with such issues to increase the likelihood of getting your customers approved — the first time.

Asking The Closing Question

"What" questions can also be used as a final closing question to signify ownership and get the paperwork started.

Ask *"What do you think about getting started today?"* or *"What would you say about getting started today?"* or *"What about going ahead and getting started today?"* or *"What about making a decision on your new home while you're here?"* or *"What other questions do you have before we get started with the paperwork?"*

———

3

———

When?

———

Future Or Past Events

Asking "when" seems like a pretty straightforward question that deals with timing — and it is.

However, there are several different types of "when" questions that you can ask to learn either the timing of future events or the history of those in the past.

Perhaps the most obvious question concerning timing is *"When do you plan on moving into your new home?"*

But it just as easily could be phrased *"When do you plan on making a decision on your new home?"*

This second question actually is the more effective one because it supplies more information.

These two questions are not the same. They are similar but can mean two entirely different things.

Avoid Asking About "Time Frame"

The question *"What's your time frame?"* is such a poor question because it tells you nothing on its face.

I think we just copy it from others because we've heard them use it, but it is a totally worthless question. *Eliminate it.*

This is a poorly disguised "when" question that doesn't work.

If you ask someone what their "time frame" is, you may think you know what you mean by asking this question, but you should be asking when they can make a decision.

Similarly, your customers may think they know what they mean when they answer your question. However, they might have several different responses in mind.

As a result, you very likely will have a miscommunication because neither one of you is *exactly* sure what is meant by the question — and maybe even less sure after it has been answered.

You may think that you are asking your customers when they are prepared to make a decision by learning when they want to move into their new home, but in order to learn this, you really need to ask specifically when they intend to make a decision on their new home.

It's The Decision Date That Matters

The *decision date* is the key to determining how you should work with a customer and how you structure your presentation.

This is the question that you need to focus on and ask.

Unless you have homes available for immediate occupancy and someone can literally make a decision today and close within a few days, when they plan on or want to move into their new home doesn't equate with a decision date.

The dates could be weeks, months, or even years apart.

What you must know is when they are capable of making a decision or how soon they intend to make it.

More On The Fallacy Of "Time Frame"

In any case, "time frame" isn't a good or meaningful question to ask. The date when someone "needs" a new home or plans on moving into it really isn't the issue.

What if "a year" is someone's "time frame" because they really don't intend to occupy their new home for a year — but they can say "yes" to their new home, give you the initial deposit, and start the paperwork *today*? Then "time frame" is irrelevant from a sales standpoint.

Put another way, what have you really learned when your customers tell you that their "time frame" is "*July*" or "*October*" or some other time designation?

What if they tell you "*3 months,*" "*a few months,*" "*within the next year,*" "*in the Spring,*" "*before Christmas,*" "*by the end of the year,*" "*before the holidays,*" "*before school starts,*" "*as soon as school gets out,*" "*after baseball (soccer, basketball, softball, hockey, football, volleyball) season,*" "*about this time next year,*" "*when we retire in another year or two,*" "*after we sell our present home,*" "*after graduation,*" "*after the wedding,*" or "*next summer*"?

Such responses really tell you nothing.

You must ask additional questions.

Don't Waste Your Questions

Why not be more specific from the beginning instead of asking a "throwaway" question like "time frame?"

If you're asking your customers about their "time frame," you're really asking a question that provides no clear answer. Ask what you really want to know.

Your customers may think they know what you're asking when you talk about time frame and tell you what they think is an appropriate response, but you probably won't know what they mean by their answer without asking additional questions — because there are so many possible answers depending on how your customers interpret this question.

Therefore, avoid this question and ask for the specific information that you want.

Getting A Useful Answer

You can't know exactly what your customers mean to a question about "time frame" or many other issues without asking additional questions that will provide clarity and more useful information.

For instance, their answer to a question about the timing of moving into their new home could mean that they plan on occupying their new home in July or the time period that they mention — without considering the time that it takes to build a home or to get one completed that is under construction.

It could also mean that they intend to make a decision on something that already exists so that they can move into it in within a few days of their decision.

They could be planning on making a decision on a home to-be-built for delivery at a later date — or getting their present home ready to put on the market or actually putting it on the market at that time.

They might mean that they are waiting until that date to "officially" start looking for a new home and that they will sell their current home later, or that this is when they will be closing on the sale of their current home.

It could be that their lease expires then and that they will begin looking for something seriously then — or that they will be getting a raise or promotion then and that they can make a decision on a new home after that time. It could mean that they are getting married then, or that they are having a baby around that time.

To-Be-Built Or Completed Home

To learn "when" your customers plan on doing something, you need to ask more than one question.

Just getting the decision date is not sufficient either because this doesn't answer all of your questions.

When you ask them when they plan on making a decision and they say *"July"* or something less specific (*"in a couple of months"*) you need to know if they plan on having you build their new home or if they want a completed (or substantially completed) home.

Depending on your construction schedule, homesite inventory, and the number of homes completed or nearly completed, you can then work with the timing that they indicate.

There's No Time Like Today

Just because someone says that they intend to make a decision *"in a few weeks"* or *"next month"* or *"after the first of the year"* or *"within a year"* doesn't necessarily mean that the decision has to wait that long.

It could actually be made the day that you're asking the question — or the next day.

Doesn't *"within a year"* include *"today"*?

The customer who gives this type of response is just indicating that they *think* that they are not close to making a decision. They really haven't focused on it.

However, you don't know just exactly what they think needs to happen before they can say "yes" to getting started on their new home.

They may be more prepared to make a decision than they think.

Depending on how long it takes to build one of your homes, it might be a year before they can move into their new home anyway — even if they say "yes" today.

Even when people think that their decision date is far off, you might be able to ask some other questions to reveal that it can be made much sooner.

Learning About Pending Events

The "when" question can also help you learn about other pending events.

"When (What day) are you planning on listing your home (putting it on the market)?" or *"When does your lease expire?"* or *"When do you think you'll be visiting our area?"* or *"When are you returning to our area?"* or *"When are you returning home?"* or *"When can we schedule a return visit?"*

"When" questions help you clarify these and other future events, such as when a missing spouse or family member is going to be available, when they start their new position, when their transfer or promotion becomes official, when they are expecting delivery of their baby, when their son or daughter is graduating or returning from military service or getting married, or when they think they will know for sure what they want in a new home or floor plan.

Using Related Questions

Often, a "when" question can be asked using other styles of questions such as asking "what" needs to happen before they can make a decision or asking them to justify or explain their reasoning with a "why" question — as in "why" they are waiting for a particular event to occur before making a decision or "why" they would want to forestall a decision that seems to be in their best interest to make now.

Finding Out About Historical Events

"When" questions can cover events that have already happened that might affect, impact, or contribute to their decision to own one of your new homes.

You can learn about the choices they made in their current home when they decided to acquire it, or when they determined that they needed to look for a new home.

You can ask about their experiences or what they remember from when they previously visited your community or drove through without stopping in, when they telephoned your community for information (if they didn't speak with you), when they looked at your ad or website, when they visited your community with a friend or relative, and when they visited other builders or resale homes in your area.

Determining Future Contact Dates

"When" questions help you plan future contact.

Initially you'll want to talk by phone to everyone — or nearly everyone — after their presentation with you, and you'll want to determine when that will occur.

Usually you'll suggest a time, but you can ask your customers for their input in selecting the appropriate day or time for you to speak with them again.

There is absolutely nothing improper about asking your customers for their input for a future contact. Getting them involved in choosing what should happen next — or a date for it to happen — includes them in the process.

You don't necessarily have to agree with what they suggest — or the time or date — but this will give you a good idea of how receptive they are and how interested they might be in what you have to offer.

Rather than a sign of weakness, this interaction is quite strategic on your part.

4

Where?

Responses Tend To Be Factual

Unless you get a vague response like *"I don't know,"* *"I don't care,"* *"I'm not sure,"* *"It doesn't matter,"* or *"It depends,"* the "where" questions that you'll ask will tend to be more factual and have more specific responses than some of the other discovery questions.

The answers usually involve a definite location or a place.

Someone might be talking about a type of neighborhood (gated, amenities, 55+), a general setting, the area, or the actual type of homesite they want.

Sometimes it may be easier for people to express "where" by telling you where they don't want to live. People will know what they don't care for or what they want to avoid, but they may not be able to express specifically what they want in a location or homesite.

They may not know what's actually available so they may have difficulty answering the "where" question.

"Where' Questions Are Versatile

In addition to being factual (*"Where do you live now?"* or *"Where do you want to live?"*), "where" questions can reference a past event, indicate a preference, or point to a planned future event.

For instance, you can ask someone where they went on their vacation last summer, where they ate dinner last night, or where they went to college — all historical questions and responses.

You can ask people where they like to go to relax or unwind, where their favorite vacation spot is, or where they would like to go for a particular activity — questions about preferences.

You also can learn where people plan on going for the holidays, where they are going this weekend, or where they are going to live when they retire — questions and discussions about future events.

Learning About Location

In your new home sales discovery, "where" questions allow you to ask historical questions about their current home that may tell you something about their search for a new neighborhood — in terms of what was important to them when they made their earlier decision and how that might relate to their current needs.

You can ask where they lived before moving into their present home — in terms of the type of home or living arrangement (lived with parents, attended school, served in the military, rented an apartment, or owned another home) and where that was (city, region, state, neighborhood, or area).

You can also ask where they live now (since this is a decision that was made in the past).

You can learn where else they have looked for a new home (other builders or neighborhoods) or where else they plan on looking or think they still need to look for a new home.

Resources Used To Locate You

"Where" questions obviously will help you define your competition by telling you where else they have looked for a new home or where they still intend to look, but they also are useful for learning "how" your traffic was generated or "why" they are looking at your homes or your particular location.

You can ask questions about where they saw your ad or message (and "why" they were looking there or "how often" they use that resource), where they heard about you (if it was from a friend, broker, or resident), or where they typically look for information about real estate or new homes.

Determining Preferences

To learn about preferences that will help you with trial closes or in selecting a specific floor plan, design, or homesite with your customers, you can use various "where" questions to ask about how they intend to use or live in their new home.

For instance, as you are showing a model home, you can ask your customers where they spend the majority of their family time together (what room or area of the home) or where the kids (if they have children) like to hang out.

You can also ask where they'd like more space than they currently have, or where (in what area of the home) they like to entertain or gather.

Using "Nesting"

An emotional selling technique that causes your customers to visualize living in the home that you are showing them and makes owning it more imaginable is called *"nesting."* This allows them feel like they are already living in the home.

Furniture placement is part of this and is a good topic to explore with your customers to help them visualize or imagine living in your floor plans and making what they are looking at or experiencing seem like their new home.

Ask them where they would place certain furniture in various rooms (such as in the living room, family room, dining room, den, or bedrooms) or how their furniture would fit along various walls.

If the home you are showing them has many places for storage (such as closets, built-in shelves or cabinets, attic, basement, garage), ask them where they would store seasonal items (water skis, snow skis, winter clothes, Christmas decorations, lawn chairs, patio furniture, and barbeque equipment).

Personalization

Get your customers involved in owning the home you are showing them by asking where they would like to have changes in the floor plan — if you allow them — such as making a certain room (or even more than one) larger, bumping-out a wall, moving a window or making it larger, adding a window or changing the style of it, or just creating more space.

Determine where your customers would like to have additional features such as a carpeting or padding upgrade, hardwood floors, tile or marble floors, wall mirrors, french doors instead of sliders, more or different appliances or lighting, more outlets or low-voltage stations, crown molding or other trim, cabinet or door hardware upgrades, countertop material or styling upgrades, or changes to the baths.

Find out where they want to create emphasis or drama in accessorizing or personalizing their home (by using customized paint, wallpaper, faux finishes, niches, columns, molding accents, built-ins, or other features).

These are great trial closing questions to use to get people to commit to a floor plan that they want to own.

Similar Approach For Started Homes

These same questions about furniture placement, planned or potential use of the floor space, and any changes they would like to make to personalize a particular home for themselves also can be used when you are showing your customers a home that is under construction or nearly completed.

You can determine where they would like to make any changes in the home that are reasonable, feasible, and still able to be accommodated.

Many of these same kinds of questions also can be used in showing a completed home that is ready for immediate occupancy.

Preferences About The Setting

Using "where" questions to determine preferences can be applied to the overall setting or location of where someone wants to live. These parallel and complement some of the "what" questions that were discussed in Chapter 2.

For instance, where — in either a general or specific sense — does someone want to live (and raise their family if they have children)?

Where in your general neighborhood or community would they like to live?

Do they want to be in a large master planned community with several recreational amenities like golf, tennis, swimming, fitness, dining, and trails? Or a smaller swim and tennis community?

Do they want to be in a certain school district?

If they're older, do they want an adult community (designated over 55 with no children)?

Do they want or are they looking for security or a maintenance-free lifestyle?

Are they looking for an area of larger homesites (an acre or more)?

Preferences About The Homesite

For the homesite, start by learning where in your community they would like to live (backing up to the preserve or open space, on the lake or golf course, near the park or amenities, on the main road, on a cul-de-sac, on a corner, on a larger than normal homesite, one with a certain orientation or view, or one with special characteristics like wooded, flat, or hilly).

This can be a great question as to "where" in the community people would like to live — in terms of the view, surroundings, or the size of the homesite premium.

Other Location Considerations

If you build off-site, on land you already own or that you will get for your customers, find out where they would like to live or where they have been looking.

If your customers already own their homesite, determine where it is located, its characteristics, and what they would like to accomplish on it.

For townhomes or condominiums, a few different "where" questions are important — where in the community (on the park, on the water, near the pool), where in the development schedule (which phase), and where in the building (which floor, which location, which orientation) do they want to live?

Determining Motivations For Moving

"Where" questions might offer or explain motivations for moving — especially if people are planning on moving to a location that is more convenient for them than where they live now.

They might want to live closer to relatives, nearer to children's activities, a few minutes from the airport, or have a quicker commute (or even live within bicycling or walking distance) to or from their employment.

Learning About Activities

You can use your "where" questions to learn about the lifestyle interests and requirements of your customers. Find out where they work, where their kids go to school, and where they like to go boating, fishing, camping, hiking, biking, or jogging.

Ask where their favorite restaurant is located in the area, where they go to church (if it comes up), and where they keep their boat or camper (or where they will need to keep it if they don't have a current facility).

Making The Decision

A great question that transcends historical, preference, and future perspectives of the "where" question is the one that learns how close they are to a decision.

This question asks *"Where are you in your thought process as far as deciding on a new home?"* or *"Where do you (you guys, you folks) stand as far as making a decision on your new home?"* or *"Where do you think you are as far as making up your mind (minds) on a new home for yourself (yourselves)?"*

"Where do you think you are as far as actually deciding on a floor plan that will work for you?" or *"Where are you as far as actually settling on a floor plan that you want to own and call 'home'?"* or *"How close are you to actually settling on a place where you want to live and call 'home'?"*

Then you can work with the answers to these questions to continue building the sale.

———

5

———

Why?

———

The Most Basic Question

Asking "why" is a very common question.

Children learn very early in life to question anything going on around them that they don't understand, and usually "why" is an inherent part of their questions.

"Why" is reflexive. It can stand by itself as a total question.

It can be used in conjunction with most other discovery questions, and it can be an add-on to any question.

Don't Oveuse

"Why" questions are great when you want to learn about someone's motivation, what they're thinking, how deeply they hold an attitude or opinion, or when you need clarification or additional information — but be careful.

"Why" questions easily can be overdone and become very tedious and boring.

You literally — like a small child — can ask "why" after almost anything that is said by your customers.

Some people can't or don't want to verbalize their rationale or thinking about a particular home or features that you're asking them about, and they can become defensive rather than open about sharing their opinions.

"Why" — In Other Words

As with other discovery questions, you can vary the wording you use to elicit an explanation — in addition to the ones where you specifically start the question with the word "why" or use the word "why" as part of your question.

You can ask *"Why do you feel that way?"* or *"Why is that?"* or *"Can you tell me why?"*

However, you can also use *"Would you please explain,"* or *"I don't think I understand,"* or *"I'm not sure what you mean by that,"* or *"Could you please elaborate?"*

Your customers just need to understand and appreciate that you're asking them for more information or an explanation or elaboration of what they've just said or expressed.

Often, an *"Oh?"* or *"Really?"* — or a surprised or questioning look or expression by you (such as raised eyebrows, a quizzical look, a slightly open mouth, or a tilt of your head) after their comment — will serve the same purpose as asking a "why" question.

The important part of using a "why" or "why"-type question is that you get people to give you more information to support or explain their response, opinion, reasoning, feelings, or logic.

Motivating Influences

In addition to asking introductory discovery questions like *"Why are you looking for a new home?"* or *"Why are you thinking of (planning on) moving?"* or *"Why did you decide to visit us today?"* there are many other "why," "why not," and "why"-type questions that you can use — to learn about someone's motivation and interest in seeking a new home.

Often, one "why" question will lead to another "why" question — or a "how" or "what," for instance — for an explanation or clarification.

You can ask someone why they chose the home they have now (including its location), why they believe it no longer meets their needs, and what they are looking for in terms of a floor plan, layout, and a particular location or area.

Maybe their planned move is based on relocating, and you can learn why they are moving to your city, area, or neighborhood — and possibly what their goals and aspirations are in a new location.

You can ask why they have chosen this particular time (in general or specifically this day) to look for a new home, or why they identified you to visit and consider for their new home.

Resales And Competition

Find out if they are interested in a new home rather than a resale.

If they are indifferent or undecided, learn why. If they definitely have ruled out existing homes in favor of a new home, also find out why so you can build upon this.

Determine why they have chosen some builders, communities, or neighborhoods to look at and rejected others — especially your direct competition.

Learn what their experiences have been in looking at those other homes and locations and why they determined that their needs couldn't be met at those other places.

"Why" questions get to the heart of what someone is looking for in a new home and how well they think it meets their needs. It allows you to compare various floor plans with them and determine their opinions.

Continuing To Look

A key issue in helping someone decide on a new home is learning why they are still in the market and continuing to look for a new home.

This can be because they have not been able to find a floor plan anywhere that will meet their needs, they have been disappointed with what they have seen at other builders, or they are just getting started in their search for a new home.

It could be a reluctance to make a decision or a basic fear of working with a builder.

Measuring Preferences

"Why" questions are great for learning attitudinal or lifestyle preferences — such as why they like or dislike something you are showing them or what they saw elsewhere (at another builder or in a resale home).

You can determine why certain included features are important to them while others are not. You also can learn why various non-included features — either available or not offered by you — might be desirable and how that might impact their decision.

As far as appearance and exterior architectural design elements, certain features and treatments may be important to your customers while others are not.

You can learn their opinions on features such as columns, arches, brick, accents, trim, banding, window placement and style, garage location, style and number of garage doors, entry door, siding, lighting, roofline, roof pitch, roofing materials, landscaping, curb appeal, and similar components.

Asking "why" questions can help you eliminate various floor plans and features from consideration.

When your customers don't like certain plans that you have, you can focus on helping them select another floor plan that will meet their needs well enough for them to make a purchasing decision to own it.

Deciding On The Exact Home To Own

In addition to learning what your customers are looking for in a floor plan or layout, asking them why they like, prefer, or favor something they remark about — or learning how strongly they dislike something — will help you to focus on a specific plan or design that they will want to own.

When you get a more complete picture of their feelings and attitudes about what you are showing them or how they feel a particular floor plan will serve their needs, you can move forward to selecting the exact home and homesite or location for them to own.

When it comes time to focus on selecting a specific floor plan, you can ask them why or how well they like a particular layout — or prefer it to something else they may have seen or considered.

Clarifying Other Issues

"Why" questions can help provide answers, explanations, opinions, and attitudes concerning other parts of your presentation.

For instance, as you begin your on-site sales presentation you learn who all of the people are in the customer unit that are present with you in your model center.

Then you might discover that at least one family member or decision-maker or influencer is absent.

From that, you can attempt to learn why the influencers or other family members are missing from the presentation or what prevented them from being present — and if they are likely to be present on a future visit.

You also can learn why someone needs to be consulted, what they can contribute to the process, and how their input or influence will affect your customer's decision.

As you find out what someone is looking for in a new home — including the features that are important to them — you can discover why particular features, design, layout, style, or location are desirable.

Conversely, you can learn what is not important to them — and why.

Facilitating The Close

When you narrow their search to just a specific home or floor plan — and they express more than just a passing interest in that home or floor plan — you can reinforce their interest and excitement level by exploring why it works so well for them.

Learn why they feel it meets their needs better than or to the exclusion of everything else they have seen.

This will lead to the final close.

You can continue with why they are looking forward to living in your community and to owning and living in their new home that they'll be getting from you.

You may need to ask what it will take or what needs to happen before they can make a decision (such as selling their present home or putting it on the market), and you can clarify their response by learning more about why that is important or why they feel it needs to happen.

Teaming Up With Other Questions

You'll find that a strategically asked "why" question will work with any of your other discovery questions.

While the "who," "what," "when," "where," "how," and "which" questions also are important to your discovery, well-timed "why" questions can go right along with them to help you understand the reasoning and the emotions behind the answers more fully and completely.

Often, the "why" will provide the necessary insight to explain answers to other questions.

Working With Objections

"Why" is a great question to use when your customers raise objections or issues — about something you're showing them or for not going ahead with a decision that seems to already be made.

In addition to finding out what the issue or concern is that they are raising, you can ask them why this issue is important, why they hold that opinion, or why they feel this way — and you can learn how strongly they hold that opinion or viewpoint.

When people want to "think about" what you've presented to them, they try to put off making a decision altogether, or they give you some other reason for not proceeding, you can ask them why they would need more time. Then you can help them clarify the reasons why they should make a decision now.

As you review with them all of the reasons why they liked what you were showing them and how this meets and solves the needs they've expressed, you can ask them why they would want to wait and possibly miss out on an opportunity that is ready for them to act on right now.

6

How?

Measuring An Amount Or Opinion

The "how" and the related "how much," "how soon," "how long," and "how often" questions request mostly factual or quantitative information from your customers — even if it's just an educated guess on their part.

"How" and "how"-type questions may also call for an opinion or explanation, but often a definite answer is what you want.

You also can use "how" or related questions such as "how well," "how much," "how strongly" or "how important" questions to measure attitudes, acceptance, or preferences.

You might be interested in the degree of certainty or conviction that someone has about a particular position or belief — or how plausible something might seem to them.

For instance, you could ask, *"How important is it for you to have ...?"* or *"How do (would) you feel about ...?"* or *"How about ...?"* or *"How strongly do you feel about ...?"* or *"How would (does) this work for you?"*

An Introductory Question

The "how" question is one of the first that you will ask in your initial discovery with a customer — whether it's a phone conversation or a visit to your model center.

You will want to know how they heard about or learned about your company or your community.

After greeting your customers, introducing yourself, and learning who they are, you'll ask a beginning question such as *"How did you hear (learn) about us?"* or *"How did you hear (learn) about (name of your company, community — or both)?"* or *"How did you happen to hear (learn) about us?"*

"How" Leads To Other Questions

After your customers tell you how they learned about or heard about you, you'll want to know more.

While you're interested in the factual answer to your question — website, newspaper ad, sign, referral, real estate agent, or some other source — you are interested in learning why that source was used.

You also want to know how important or influential that source was in prompting their visit, what specifically it was in your message that caused them to decide to visit you, and if they also used other sources to learn about you besides the ones they mentioned.

If they tell you that they visited your website, then you'll want to learn more about how that happened — *"How did you learn about our website?"* or *"Do you remember what you saw on our website that stood out as important to you?"*

Learning About Their Online Search

If you determine that they learned about your homes or initially located you online, you can ask about "how" they conducted their online search, which search engines they may have used, and what key words or phrase they used with *"How did you search for our site or happen to locate it?"* or *"What phrase (key words) did you use for your search when you found our website?"* or *"What site did you start with to link to (find) us?"*

You'll also want to know if they used anything else in addition to your website to learn about and locate you — a sign, one of your ads, or talking with someone who has visited your model or lives in one of your homes.

If they answer that they saw a newspaper ad, you can ask *"What in particular in the ad caught your attention (was important to you)?"* or *"Do you remember what stood out in our ad that caught (attracted) your attention (eye)?"* or *"What did you notice as being important to you that was in our ad?"*

What you're trying to learn is how important the ad was in connecting with them or in prompting their visit.

There may be other aspects of your print ad that you'll want to ask about also, such as the day they saw it, if they've seen any of your other ads (and where and when — as well as what the ads may have featured, if they recall), and how often they look at that publication for real estate information.

Finding Out About Other Sources

Similar types of "how" questions can be used for other sources that people may have used.

If they say that a sign attracted their visit, a good question is *"Are you looking for homes in this area?"*

You can also ask *"Are you looking to relocate to this area (neighborhood, community)?"* or *"Do you recall why (how) you noticed our sign?"* or *"How long have you been looking for a home in this area?"* or *"How often have you driven through this area looking for a new home?"* or *"How long have you been driving around in this area looking for a new home?"*

When a friend, relative, co-worker, or acquaintance told them about you, ask *"What specifically did your friend tell you about us that made you want to visit us?"* or *"Have they visited us recently?"* or *"Do they already live in (own) one of our homes?"*

Questions Are Interchangeable

Asking someone about how they located or learned about you does double-duty.

It explains which source or sources they used to locate or learn about you prior to visiting, and it provides a reason why they have chosen to visit you at this time — or an opportunity for you to learn this.

It may also tell you or indicate what is important for your customers to find in a builder, floor plan or layout, home design, included features, pricing, amenities, lifestyle, financing, or location.

By now, you should appreciate the inter-relationship of questions and that there often are several ways of asking for similar or essentially the same type of information.

Indicating Preferences And Intent

After showing your customers your available homes or floor plans, you can ask questions about how well your homes address certain issues or meets their needs.

"How" questions make great trial closing questions —and even transition into the final close — because they invite a qualitative response or ask for a preference among various choices or options.

For instance, *"How does this floor plan work for you?"* or *"How do you feel about this floor plan?"* or *"What do you think of this floor plan?"* or *"How does this compare to what you had in mind (for your new home)?"* or *"How well does this compare to other homes you've looked at?"* or *"How does this compare to what you have now?"*

Or you can ask *"How well does this address (compare to) what you've been looking for in a new home?"* or *"How well does this floor plan solve (address or eliminate) the issues that you're dealing with in your current home?"*

For a more specific closing question you can ask: *"Do you think that this is the type of home that you would like to own?"* or *"What part of this home do you like the best?"* or *"Which part of this home (floor plan) appeals to you the most?"*

You could also ask "nesting" and preference questions during your presentation, such as *"How would you arrange your furniture in this room?"* or *"Where would you put your couch (TV, recliners, hutch, entertainment center) in this room?"* or *"How well do you think your wife/husband (not present) would like this layout (kitchen, family room, deck, pool, basement, patio)?"*

For deciding on important features, you can ask *"How important is it for your new master bath to have a jacuzzi (whirlpool, soaking tub)?"* or *"How important is having a children's playroom?"* or *"How important is it for you to have a quiet area away from the family where you can work on your novel (paperwork)?"*

Accenting The Lifestyle

The "how" question is a good one to use if you are selling in an amenitized community (such as golf, tennis, swimming, fitness, clubhouse, or dining).

Use this type of question to determine the relative importance of having those activities available and to reinforce the presence of those facilities in your presentation.

You can focus on the view with *"How would you like to enjoy an evening cocktail or glass of wine sitting on this beautiful veranda overlooking the 17th fairway?"* or *"How hard would it be to come home to this gorgeous view each night?"*

To help your customers develop an emotional attachment for what you are offering, ask about usage patterns for the areas they really like, such as *"How frequently do you think you might use ...?"* or *"How often do you think you might take advantage of the ...?"* or *"How do you think your kids would like having ...?"*

Creating Tie-Downs

You can expand your use of the "how" and "how"-type questions to help you illustrate specific aspects of your floor plans and cause your customers to become more emotionally attached to what you are showing them.

You might ask questions such as *"How often do you bring work home at night and need a quiet or dedicated space where you can work on business without being interrupted by other family members?"* or *"How often do you think you might be using your new kitchen (pool area, family room, deck, enclosed patio, sunroom) for entertaining?"*

You might focus on an aspect of the floor plan with *"How many steps do you think it might save by having the laundry room right next to the bedrooms instead of near (in) the garage?"* or *"How many people do you think you can seat (entertain, host) for Thanksgiving dinner in this spacious dining room?"*

Of Degrees And Amounts

"How" questions are useful for getting opinions, but they also are great for creating contrasts, providing comparisons, or asking rhetorical questions.

They help get your customers to project or imagine how they might use certain rooms or features of the new home you are showing them — or to consider comfort and convenience aspects of the floor plan.

Measuring With "How Much"

"How much" questions are good to use when you are looking for a time or usage response — or an amount of money.

Ask your customers about how much time they have for a presentation on this visit, how much home they are looking for, how much they are intending to invest in their new home, how much they intend to finance on their new home, how much of an initial deposit they are planning, or how much initial equity they would like to create in their new home.

Learning Timing With "How Soon

There also are "how soon" questions that allow you to gauge a time component for a future event from your customers.

Learn how soon they want to act, how soon they are prepared to make a decision, or how soon they are capable of making one and getting started.

Determine how soon they plan on selling their current home or putting it on the market, or how soon their lease expires.

Find out how soon they start their new job, or how soon their promotion or transfer becomes official.

Then, there is how soon they would like to move into their new home. This might revolve around the school year, holidays, or other events in their lives.

Using "How Long" To Focus

The "how long" question is related and can be used interchangeably with the "how soon" question to measure time.

You can ask your customers how long before they'll know specifically what they want in a floor plan, how long before they put their home on the market, or how long before they start their new position.

You can ask them how long they have been looking for a new home, how much longer they plan on continuing to look at new homes, or how long they want to wait before beginning to enjoy their new home.

Similarly, you can ask how long (how much time) they have for your initial presentation, how long before they are ready to make a decision, how long (how much longer) they are willing to go on living in a home that no longer meets their needs, and how long they want to continue commuting from their current home that is no longer convenient for them.

Since they may not be aware of "how long" it takes to produce a new home — their decision date may actually be much sooner than they had anticipated.

Making Direct Comparisons

"How" questions — even if they don't begin with the word "how" — are useful for making direct comparisons.

You can ask questions beginning with "how" or you can ask your customers to "compare" or "contrast" a floor plan, layout, design, or feature that you're presenting to them with something else they've seen, experienced, thought about, or imagined.

This could involve the competition, what they have now, or what you are showing them.

As you are orienting them to your community or neighborhood, comparisons are important.

You can find out how you compare with other places that they have looked at, or with what they had in mind for the layout, design, floor plan, features, setting, or homesite choices for their new home.

When you show your model or a specific available home, you can ask how they think you can meet their needs better than anything else they have seen — or what they think might be available if they continue to look.

Learn how you compare with what they thought you would be, or how you compare to what they currently have.

Forming Conclusions

"How" and "how"-type questions can cause your customers to focus on why something is important to them, explain how they might use their new home, or justify certain features they want to have.

They also help your customers to decide on a specific floor plan and begin the process of acquiring that new home from you.

"How" questions help you learn if something is important to your customers — and the degree of importance or emphasis that they place on it.

They allow your customers to explain why they like or dislike something.

"How" questions really get to the core of making a sale.

7

Which?

The Ultimate Choice Question

"Which" is a great question because it calls for a conclusion — a decision.

When used correctly, there is no doubt that you're asking someone about their preference, choice, or selection.

For instance, *"Which one do you like, 'A' or 'B'?"* or *"Which one do you prefer?"* or *"Which one would you like to have (own)?"* or *"Which one have you selected?"* or *"Which one have you decided on?"*

A Question Of Recall

You also can use a "which" question to ask about a recollection or for a recall, as in *"Which one did you see (look at)?"* or *"Which one was it?"* or *"Do you remember (recall) which one?"* or *"Which one had ...?"*

However, this type of question doesn't work well — and really shouldn't be used — with people who don't make decisions easily, who really don't know what they want, who aren't particularly observant, who don't want to commit themselves, or who can't or won't recall what they've seen.

In those cases, you'll get an answer like *"I don't know,"* *"I'm not sure,"* *"I need more time to think about it,"* *"I really didn't pay (wasn't paying) any attention to it (that),"* *"It depends,"* *"I really can't say (for sure),"* or *"I don't (can't) remember."*

Don't Force It

Sometimes, when you ask people for their preference, you'll get the ultimate ambiguous response which is *"I like (liked) them all"* or *"I like (liked) all of them."*

You should only ask for a decision or a selection — a "which one" choice — after you have given your customers some specific examples or you know that they have enough information and experience to be able to answer your question.

If there is any concern that someone is confused or has not made up their mind on a floor plan, design, feature, location, or view that you have shown them — or that it is unlikely that they can express their opinion or choice — the "which" question won't give a specific answer.

In that case, go for a little clarification, as in *"Which one are you leaning toward?"* or *"Which one do you think you prefer?"* or *"If you had to make a choice, which one do you feel the strongest (best) about?"*

Even here, you may not get a definitive response.

Reflexive Questions

Asking a "which" question should get almost an automatic response — one that people don't have to pause and think about too much before they answer.

To get your customers used to answering either a specific choice question or a recall question — and to find out how well they can respond to a "which" question — you can give them a couple of easy ones in the beginning of your presentation.

Set up a little test to determine if they are comfortable answering "which" or "which"-type questions.

For instance, in the early part of your on-site presentation or incoming telephone call with someone, you might ask *"Which newspaper did you see our ad in?"* or *"Which day was that?"* or *"Which search engine did you use to find our website?"*

Here you'll get either a specific response or an *"I don't know"* or *"I don't remember"* or *"I'm not sure."*

When they say that they don't remember — or they don't appear to try very hard to remember — this might signal a general low level of interest in getting a new home, in getting one from you, or in being able to make any type of decision.

It could mean a general lack of cooperation or unwillingness to share information with you.

It also could mean that they really don't remember, that it didn't matter that much to them for them to make a point of specifically remembering it, or that they aren't very good at remembering details.

Nevertheless, there is no right or wrong, or good or bad answer to a "which" question — you're only asking for information and for people to reveal a preference, choice, or selection.

Getting Market Information

"Which" questions can help you learn about your competition.

For instance, you can ask someone about a location, neighborhood, community, or builder with *"Which other places (communities, areas, builders, neighborhoods) have you looked at (visited, considered) so far?"* or *"Which other places are you still planning on (thinking about) visiting (looking at)?"*

You can ask about floor plans or layouts that they have seen and evaluated — *"Which floor plans have you seen that are kind of close to what you are looking for?"* or *"Which floor plans that you've looked at so far are the closest to being what you're looking for in a new home?"* or *"Which homes have you seen so far that you kind of like?"* or *"Which homes have you looked at so far that you think might work for you?"*

These questions are asked as much to help you learn about your competition as they are to help you focus on working with a specific customer.

Getting A Jump Start

If you determine that they've seen your website or mention having seen a floor plan in one of your ads, you could ask *"Which floor plan did you like?"* or *"Which floor plan looks like it will work for you?"* or *"Which one do you like the best?"* or *"Which exterior design do you like the best (prefer)?"*

This can help you decide which plan to suggest to them, discuss with them, or show them *first*.

Asking The Closing Question

The "which" questions — above all the others you can ask — lead to the actual final decision because they indicate ownership.

This is a definitive question that calls for a choice, such as *"Which floor plan do you prefer?"* or *"Of what we have looked at today, which floor plan (home) do you think you would like to own?"* or *"Which of these 2 (3) floor plans that we've looked at is the one you'd like to own?"* or *"Which one would you like to own (live in)?"*

Then you can get specific about which homesite or location they want to own — leading ultimately to the final closing question.

Setting Up Trial Closes

As you narrow your focus on "which" floor plan, design, or layout your customers would like to own, there are various choices that you can ask them to make as trial closing questions.

You can clarify floor treatments, wall and trim paint, cabinet styles, hardware, molding packages, appliances, fixtures, countertops, lighting, and other included or available features where you offer or make available more than one brand, grade, style, finish, or color.

After showing or explaining a couple of different possibilities or choices in finishes, colors, or styles — either included features or ones the customers can select — you can confirm which one they like or prefer for you to include in their new home. Make notes on what they selected and use it to write the agreement.

For example, *"Which cabinet style do you prefer, the smooth front or the raised panel?"* or *"Do you like the raised panel doors or the smooth?"* or *"Which floor tile do you think you would want installed, the 16 inch or the 24 inch?"* or *"Which wall would you want us to do in here (the family room or living room that you're standing in with them) in the accent color?"*

These questions help your customers identify with the home you're showing them, cause them to visualize it as being their own, and make it possible to close on the entire sale eventually.

As long as they are making choices, they are becoming more involved with owning that home.

Asking "Which" In Other Ways

As with other types of discovery questions, "which" and "which"-type questions don't always need the word "which" in them.

For instance, *"How do you feel about a golf course location?"* or *"Do you want a golf course location (homesite)?"* are just other ways of asking *"Which homesite (location) do you like (want, prefer)?"* or *"Which one appeals to you?"* or *"Do you like (prefer, want, favor) this one or the other one we just looked at?"* or *"Is this the homesite (location) you'd like to own (have your new home on)?"*

Making Additional Selections

As you are doing the paperwork and noting their selections, there will come time for asking your customers which view, architectural design, roof color, roofing type, exterior siding or finish, exterior color, orientation, and other pertinent items they want to select for their new home.

You also will want to determine which additional features they want to put in their new home to personalize it.

Some of this you may already have covered and noted earlier in your presentation.

Another important series of "which" questions will focus on which type of financing, which specific financing plan, and which lender they will want to use.

Selling Their Current Home

If you have learned that their present home is on the market, that they are going to be listing it soon, or that they need to sell it before making a buying decision with you, a good question to ask is "how" they are going to sell their current home.

If they are going to be selling it themselves, ask them *"Which resources have you identified to help you* advertise and promote the sale of your home?" or "How do you plan on making people aware of the fact that you're selling your home?" or "How long do you think it might take you to sell your home on your own?"

If they tell you that they are using a broker or mention that their home is on the market or already listed, ask them a question such as "Which agent have you listed your home with?" or "Which real estate agent (office) are you going to be working with?" or "Which broker have you selected to market your current home?"

If they are only in the planning stages for selling their current home or you detect that even though they say they want to sell their own home that they may not be fully committed to getting the job done on their own and could be open to talking with an agent, you can ask "Which real estate agents have you talked to (with) about selling your current (present) home for you?" or "Do you know any agents that you could talk to about your present home?" or "Which broker are you thinking of calling (using) to help you sell your current home?" or "Which real estate agent are you planning on talking to (with) about helping you sell your current home?"

The Broker Connection

When you learn which real estate sales professional your customers are using to sell their current home, you can reach out to that agent and let them know that you have a new home sale pending for your customers based on their ability to sell the customer's current home.

This is not to create any type of pressure on the listing agent but only to open a line of communication and assistance. Offer any kind of support that you can to help get this home sold.

If you happen to have a relationship with this broker already, this gives you another reason to contact and interact with him or her. If you and the agent have never spoken before, it's a chance for you to meet this person and begin developing a relationship.

If your customer is open to suggestions on which real estate salesperson to use, you can offer them the name of one or two people that you have a relationship with that you feel confident can sell their home quickly and respect the pending sale that you have.

You can rotate or vary the names of the brokers you hand out depending on how many agents you are comfortable referring to your customers.

Either way, this is all part your broker outreach program.

8

More Questions

Other Possibilities

So far in this book, I have been focusing on having you ask questions to elicit information from your customers by using the "who," "what," "when," "where," "why," "how," and "which" types of questions.

These are solid question formats that will serve you quite well and enable you to form a complete picture of your customers as you build a sale.

However, there are a few other ways of asking questions that I want you to be aware of to give you further discovery possibilities.

Actually, these other techniques complement the "who," "what," "when," "where," "why," "how," and "which" types of questions and give you additional power, variety, and choices for your discovery.

Yes/No Questions

We have all used "yes/no" questions throughout our lives. We have been asked such questions, and we have asked others these questions.

They definitely have a place in the sales interview — especially when you just need a confirmation or agreement.

However, if you need a more complete response, a short answer, or an explanation, the "yes/no" format is not recommended.

There will be times when you might just need a quick "yes" or "no" without any elaboration or explanation — depending on how you have phrased your question — to be able to continue with your presentation or move on to something else.

There are many examples of "yes/no" questions that you can use.

Some will totally stand alone.

Some will be a lead-in to other questions.

Examples of standalone questions — where just the "yes" or "no" answer will suffice — are ones like "*Is it still raining outside?*" or "*Are they still working on Route 7?*"

or *"Do you have time for me to show you ...?"* or *"Would you like a glass of water?"* or *"Would you care to sit down?"* or *"Do you mind if ...?"* or *"Would it be OK if ...?"*

They can be more conversational — especially at the beginning — than specifically part of your presentation.

Trial Closing Or Selection Questions

Even in the selection process or as trial closes, "yes/no" questions can be used when both you and the customer know what the answer is revealing.

They are great to get your customers to indicate a preference when it's just a matter of whether they want something or they don't — no other choices. This is just a simply matter of "yes" they like something or want it — or "no" they don't.

Occasionally, you may get a *"We're not sure,"* or *"Possibly,"* or *"It depends,"* or *"We haven't really discussed it,"* or *"We have different opinions (ideas) on that — I want it and she/he doesn't."*

Obviously you will need to ask more questions to shed some light on the ambiguity or to give you some more information on where to go with your presentation.

Examples of "yes/no" questions that you might use are *"Are you looking for a formal dining room?"* or *"Is a fireplace important to you?"* or *"Do you want each child to have their own bedroom?"* or *"Are you interested in the split bedroom plan?"* or *"Would you like a corner location?"* or *"Do you want both a shower and a tub in your master bath?"*

Sometimes — even when a "yes" or "no" can answer the question — you will get a more complete response, such as when you ask if a they want both a tub and shower in their master or if they would like a corner homesite.

They may answer *"yes"* or *"no"* and then proceed to defend their answer or tell you why this is the case. That's fine.

Questions That Lead To Another

Sometimes the "yes/no" question can be used for variety or as a lead-in to a "who," "what," "when," "where," "why," "how," or "which" type of question.

When you are beginning your presentation, you might ask someone if they saw your newspaper ad or visited your website. Regardless of the answer, you want more information, so you'll explore their response with additional questions.

You might ask someone if they like or want carpeting in the family room. If they say *"yes,"* you'll want to ask about the color, style, thickness of the pad, and grade of the carpet. If they say *"no,"* you'll want to know what type of flooring they are looking for.

You'll have many opportunities to use a "yes/no" question during your presentation for confirmation of a color, style, or grade of an included feature.

Other times, you will likely need to ask more specific questions than "yes" or "no" to determine exactly what they prefer and want to own in their new home.

Use This Tool Appropriately

The "yes/no" questions can be effective when you need a quick preference answer or don't require a longer explanation.

Just be careful not to use them too often.

The real heart of your discovery is still your "who," "what," "when," "where," "why," "how," and "which" types of questions.

If you use the "yes/no" too often, it may become tedious. Also, you will not be drawing your customers into the discussion or learning what is motivating them to want or select certain aspects of their new home — or even how prepared they are to make a decision on their new home or how well they think what you are showing them can serve their needs.

Scaling Questions For Opinions

Another type or style of question that you can use is the scaling question where you ask people to compare or contrast something you are showing them with their idea of the "perfect" solution for them — a particular feature they are considering, a floor plan you are discussing with them, or a homesite location.

In this type of question, the lower the rating the more disinterested or dissatisfied people are with something you are discussing with them. A higher number means that they are closer to accepting the premise you are offering them.

This can be a great trial closing question, but there is one significant drawback.

Scaling Question Limitations

Many people simply cannot express their feelings in a ranked or quantified response so it may have limited usefulness as a questioning technique — depending on the specific customers you are working with at the time.

Some people tend to respond with something toward the middle — regardless of what you are asking. If they really like something, they may only give you a "6" or a "7" in response. They may just stick with the "4-6" range to express "average" and let it go at that.

Then you'll have to try to interpret what they mean by asking them additional questions.

Some people are more absolute and definite in their responses — giving you a "1" or even a "0" if they really don't like it and a "9" or "10" if they are impressed.

Some people just don't like to commit themselves and will say that they are not very good at coming up with a number or answer your question with a non-numeric answer, such as *"pretty good"* or *"not bad."*

Examples Of Scaling Questions

Scaling questions ask people to compare or contrast something against, or in terms of, their ideal. This only works if they have a good idea of what they're looking for and are able to express that on a 1-10 scale. Then you'll have something to build on.

For instance, you can ask *"On a scale of 1-10, how well does this floor plan (home) meet your needs?"* or *"On a scale of 1-10, how would you rate this as the ideal floor plan for you?"* or *"On a scale of 1-10, with 10 being the absolute best, how do you rate this home as being what you're looking for?"*

Then you can focus on any responses less than a "9" or "10" with questions such as *"What would it take to make this floor plan a '9' or a '10' instead of the '7' you are giving it now?"* or *"Why do you give it just a '7' or an '8' — what is missing?"* or *"Only a '6' — it seemed like you really liked this plan?"*

The scaling question should only be used once or twice in a presentation as a serious trial closing question. It is another way of asking *"How well does this floor plan work for you?"* or *"How do you feel about (owning) this floor plan?"* or *"How does this compare to what you had in mind (for your new home)?"* or *"Is this the home you want to own?"*

Then you can address their response and continue with your presentation. You might have a sale at that point, or you might be back at the beginning — asking more questions.

Alternate-Choice Questions

In addition to asking "yes/no" questions to learn preferences, you can gather information and employ trial closes with a questioning technique called "alternate-choice."

Essentially you will be giving your customers two choices to select from — one of which you are reasonably certain they will select.

Going back to an earlier example — the one about the tub and shower in the master bath — instead of asking if it is important to have both as a "yes/no" question, you could use an alternate-choice question such as *"We can build your master bath with either the tub and the shower as you see them, or with a larger walk-in shower without the separate tub — which would you prefer?"*

This technique is useful when you offer two variations of a room layout such as the bathroom example, or when you have two choices of colors or finishes such as with appliances, fixtures, or hardware.

Getting A Definitive Answer

If you offer white and black appliance colors, and you ask you customer which one they prefer, they might say that they really wanted to have stainless steel. While that isn't an included feature — if you offer it or choose to make it available to your customers — you can mention how much additional it would be and secure agreement that they want it. Then make a note to yourself to include it on the purchase agreement.

It's possible that when you ask your customers for a choice between two colors or styles that they will ask you if that is all that is available or if they could pick something else as a custom upgrade.

Then you can discuss their available choices with them, determine exactly what they want, and make a note to include this on the purchase agreement.

Versatility Of This Technique

The alternate-choice question is a good one to intersperse in your sales interview to add variety and versatility to your trial closing and selection questions.

Sometimes your customers will indicate a specific choice from the two that you are offering, and sometimes they will ask you about additional choices. Either way, you are getting closer to a sale.

The alternate-choice does the work of a "which one" question or a "what" question — giving you the flexibility to ask questions in different ways.

The Probe

In Chapter 5, I mentioned using a raised eyebrow, a surprised or quizzical look, or an *"Oh?"* or *"Really?"* to get your customer to elaborate on what they were telling you — a variation on asking *"why?"*

Even a pause with your hand cupped around your chin — or stroking your chin — and a puzzled *"Hmmm"* can elicit an explanation.

A probe is any type of question — like these or even any of the other "who," "what," "when," "where," "why," "how," and "which" questions — where you ask for a clarification or additional information.

Other examples of probing questions or statements are *"Tell me more,"* or *"Can you elaborate?"* or *"Can you please explain what you mean?"* or *"How's that?"* or *"I don't understand,"* or *"Help me understand,"* or *"I'm not following you,"* or *"Not sure exactly what you mean (by that),"* or *"Can you be more specific?"* or *"Care to explain?"* or *"That's interesting,"* or *"Interesting that you would (should) say that."*

The Porcupine

Sometimes you won't be the one asking the questions. You'll be on receiving end temporarily. Think of a porcupine, a pineapple, or a cactus — not something you'd want to have someone throw and expect you to catch. It's sharp and prickly.

So, if someone were to throw you some thorny object like this — and you had to catch it — what would be your first inclination? To catch it as lightly as possible and to get rid of it immediately?

Keep this concept in mind for addressing many questions that you get. I'm not talking about factual ones, such as when your customers ask about the dimensions of a room or what school district your homes are in.

Rather, use this porcupine technique as a type of probe to send the question back to your customers with a question of your own.

Maybe you've heard or been told to answer a question with a question? That's what this technique is all about.

You need to use this form of questioning strategically, or it will seem trite, insincere, and overworked.

If someone asks if they can get maple cabinets — and they can — just answer the question affirmatively and confirm that this would be a choice they would select for their new home. Then make a note on your information card or tablet and continue with your presentation.

Answering Objections

Use the porcupine technique for clarification of an objection or concern that your customers might raise or ask about.

For instance, they might say something like *"Why is this homesite so small?"* Before you can even begin to answer their question, you need to know more about why they have asked this.

You can use a probe by expressing that you're not sure what they mean by their question or asking them to explain their concern.

You also can toss the question back to them with a puzzled *"Why is this homesite so small?"* or *"Homesite so small?"* or *"Small?"* to learn why they have asked this.

The "Troll"

Beware of the "troll." This is a tricky type of question that people might ask you. It's a trap so be careful.

"Troll" is a word I created to apply to this type or form of question — adapted from a similar meaning in online chats, forums, and comments.

It's not a legitimate question, but you can easily add credence to it by the way you answer it.

It begins with a premise that something is universal, when in fact, it is not. It may only be their opinion, an urban legend, or conventional wisdom. However, if you allow the premise to stand by addressing the second part of their question, you have agreed to the first part.

Someone may start with an inclusive statement like *"Everyone knows that builders are in trouble,"* or *"Everyone knows that builders are willing to negotiate,"* or *"Everyone knows that builders have plenty of room to negotiate,"* or *"Everyone knows that all new homes are overpriced."* Then they'll explain why you're not competitive or why they are entitled to a big concession.

They might also say something like *"All builders are in trouble,"* or *"All builders are giving big discounts,"* or *"All builders are open to offers (willing to negotiate),"* or *"All new homes are overpriced."*

Avoid Taking The Bait

Rather than taking the bait about "everyone knows" or "all builders," just ask *"Why do you say that?"* or *"What makes you say that?"* or *"Really?"*

Make them defend their position or explain what they are trying to accomplish by making such a statement. Then, you can work with their concern from a more factual or issue-oriented standpoint.

Also, be careful in trying to distance or differentiate your company from your competition by saying that you're not like all of the other builders or that you're different.

You won't have uncovered the reason they made the statement, and you could get deeper into discussing — or even arguing about — their claim instead of addressing their real concern or issue constructively.

Strip away the generalizations and ask questions to determine what they are looking for and how ready, willing, and able they are to make a decision.

9

Go Discover

Summary Of Question Choices

In this book, I've given you the basics of discovery — the art of getting to know who you're working with in any sales encounter and their basic needs and requirements.

This includes people walking into your model center, those calling for information on the phone, those sending in a third part-party surrogate or real estate agent to meet with you and gather information, and those who contact you by email — directly or through your website.

You start with just the introduction and go from there.

With the various questioning strategies that I've illustrated, you can learn who the various people are that are participating in the decision, what needs to happen before the decision can occur, where people are in their search process, how people located you and what their expectations are, how to determine what's important to your customers, trial closing questions that you can use to help in the selection process, and the final close that signifies ownership.

You can create relationships with your customers — more than anything else, sales are built upon and result from strong relationships.

The Inter-Relationship Of Questions

As I took you through each chapter — who, what, when, where, why, how, and which (plus the additional types of questions) — I illustrated for you how many of the questions are inter-related and how there are various ways of asking for essentially the same information.

This way, you can vary your techniques and questioning style and use what's comfortable for you and your customers.

You can keep your discovery interview with your customers fresh, and somewhat spontaneous.

For instance, you can ask someone *where* else they have looked for a new home, *what* other places they have considered, or *which* other places they have visited.

These are just various ways of requesting the same information from the customer.

Similarly, you can ask someone when they would like to move into or be living in their new home, when they intend to make a decision, how soon they would like to be in their new home, or how long before they're able to make a decision.

You also could ask them what needs to happen before they feel comfortable making a decision.

Keep The Questions Interesting

By having many different ways of asking the same basic question — or for requesting essentially the same information — you can vary the way you ask your questions.

Even with the same customer, you can ask for the same information in various ways — in case the first answer seemed incomplete or vague — or you want to verify that what they told you earlier in the presentation is still true later.

Don't feel that you need to follow a certain regimen by starting with "who" questions and going through the other types of questions we've discussed — in order.

Your presentation will develop a certain rhythm and style. There will be questions that you'll typically ask your customers at the outset of your presentation to learn who they are and what they want to accomplish, but the rest will depend on their needs, interest level, and ability to act.

So Now What?

I've given you a strategic approach to asking questions.

I've included a variety of questions and various ways to ask a similar question.

Don't feel that this is a comprehensive list of questions or that you need to adhere to these — I want you to inject your own personality and style.

They are provided as a guideline and to help you be aware of the many ways of involving your customers in the presentations you are conducting.

Besides, there will be issues raised during your presentation or your post-visit Follow-Through® that will evoke and require their own specific questions.

By using questions such as I have provided here, you'll have a great start at building a successful sales presentation, connecting with your customers, and being a more effective new home salesperson.

Steve Hoffacker

Steve Hoffacker, CAPS, MCSP, MIRM, is the manager at Hoffacker Associates LLC, a sales training (new home sales, universal design, and aging-in-place) and coaching company based in West Palm Beach, Florida.

Steve is an award-winning, internationally-recognized and experienced new home salesperson and sales trainer, as well as a universal design/aging-in-place safety and accessibility sales trainer and instructor.

For more than 30 years, he has helped homebuilders, new home salespeople, contractors and remodelers, new home marketers, designers, architects, occupational therapists, real estate sales professionals, and others to be more visible, competitive, profitable, and effective — and to really enjoy themselves as they pursue their business and create wonderful customer experiences.

Steve wants you and your company to be successful and has created this and many other books to help make that happen.

This book will be a great resource to help you take your business to another level and outpace the competition.

Use these strategies and concepts for your professional success.

www.ingramcontent.com/pod-product-compliance
Lightning Source LLC
Chambersburg PA
CBHW062005200326
41519CB00017B/4676